The Big Book of Salt and Pepper Shaker Series

Irene Thornburg

4880 Lower Valley Road, Atglen, PA 19310 USA

These sets of Precious Moments Noah's Ark animals were made for Enesco in China, although they do not carry an "Enesco" name. The display unit had to be bought separately if you purchased sets in a store. I bought the entire group as one unit. 2.25" to 4". $16-18 per set. $160-165 for the entire group, including the display rack.

The entire display.

Elephants and pigs.

Zebras and goats.

Giraffes and llamas.

Sheep and rabbits.

Mr. and Mrs. Noah.

The World Wildlife Federation had Benjamin and Medwin produce this series of endangered species. They were made in Taiwan. Some of the sets do not indicate the maker. 3.25" to 4". $15-18.

Pandas and koalas.

Owls and penguins.

African animals on a grass-like base make up this series. Marked with a red "Japan" stamp. 1.5" to 1.75". $8-10.

Leopards and tigers.

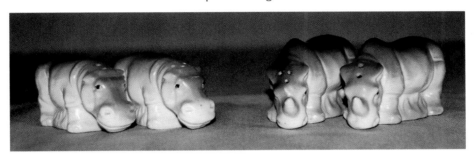

Hippos and rhinos.

Tall animals, all on an identical base. Some of these are marked from various zoos around the country. They have a blue and white "Japan" sticker. 4.75". $15-18.

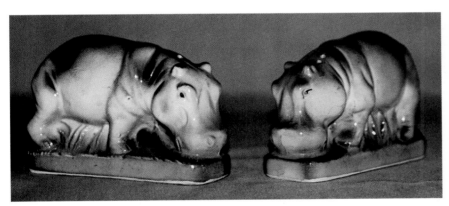

Above left: Hippos.

Left: Monkeys and gorillas (apes?).

Above right: Bears.

Dog heads. These have a paper label or a black "Japan" stamp. 2.5".
$8-10.

Boxers and Great Danes.

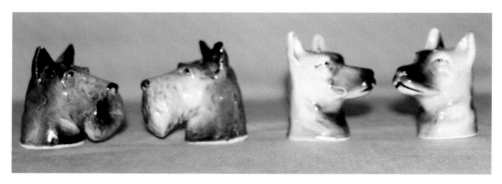

Schnauzers and Dobermans.

Collies.

Adult dogs marked with a "Victoria Ceramics–Japan" label. 3" to 3.5".
$15-18.

English Setters.

Poodles.

Pointers.

Cocker Spaniels.

Collies.

These dogs have a "Relco–Japan" sticker. The greyhound is 5.5" long, the Basset is 5" long, while the sitting dogs are 3.25" tall. Greyhounds, collies, and pointers: $18-22. Other sets: $12-15.

Greyhounds.

Basset hounds.

Dalmatians.

Boston Terriers.

Boxers.

Collies.

Dachshunds.

English Setters.

The puppies in this series closely resemble some of the dogs in the previous picture. Black and white "Enesco–Japan" label. 2.25" to 2.75". $12-15.

Cocker Spaniels and Dalmatians.

Beagles and Boxers.

Collies and Dachshunds.

More puppies. These have a "Napcoware–Japan paper label and are marked "1776." 2.75". $10-12.

Cocker Spaniels.

Collies and Dachshunds.

Some pretty kittens. Based on the markings, it is felt that they are a companion series to the puppies in the previous picture. They have a "Napcoware–Japan" paper label and are marked "1777." 3" to 3.25". $10-12.

Siamese.

Grays and Tigers.

The tags on these cats declare that they are "Kittens by Karen." If one is lucky, the tag telling the name of the kittens is still attached. Red and gold "Japan" label. 3". $20-25.

"Cutie Pie" and "Saucy."

"Cuddly" and "Merry."

"Lucky" and a single "Giggles."

Fat "roly-poly" animals are next. They have a red and gold "Japan" label. Each set has a different number stamped on it. 2.375" to 3". $10-12.

Lions marked "H956."

Foxes marked "H950" and dogs marked "H954."

Kangaroos marked "H985" and elephants marked "H955."

Animals with large spots. They have an "Enesco–Japan" label. 2.25" to 3.5". $8-10.

Rabbits.

Pigs.

Cattle.

Animals beside a stump. Each is stamped with a different number. Marked with a red and gold "Made in Japan" label. 2.5" to 3". $6-8.

Bear marked "H55."

Rabbit marked "H53" and raccoon marked "H54."

21

Large and small animals which are identical except for size. They are stamped "Murray Kreiss & Co." and have a small "Japan" label. 2" to 4" for the small sets and 2.75" to 5" for the large sets. Small sets: $10-12. Large sets: $15-18.

Dogs, look like Cocker Spaniels.

Pigs.

Donkeys.

Owls.

Bobcats??

Penguins.

Bears.

Elephants.

23

Beavers.

Monkeys.

Skunks.

Foxes.

24

These animals sit on logs that fit together. As a result, the animals appear to be kissing. They have an "Imported by Giftcraft–Toronto" label. 3.5" to 4". $10-12.

Skunks.

Squirrels and bears.

This next series features a mother with her baby in a house. They have a "Lefton–Korea" label. 2.5" to 3". $15-18.

Pigs.

Mice.

Dogs.

Animals sitting beside a stump. They have a "Bone China–Japan" red and gold label. 1.5". $8-10.

Owls.

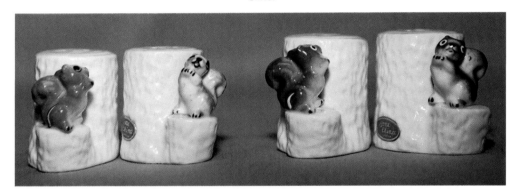

Chipmunks and squirrels.

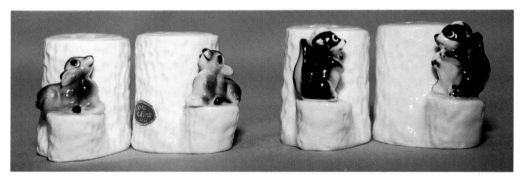

Deer and skunks.

Brown bears and black bears.

These large dressed animals are made by Ardalt in Japan. These pairs differ from those shown in an article which appeared in the August, 1991 issue of the Novelty Salt and Pepper Shakers Club newsletter. They were placed together for these photos based on logical pairings. 6". $40-45.

Frog and hippo.

Elephant and lion.

Dog and cat.

Umbrellas are the common feature in this series. They have no marks. 5".
$45-50.

Pig and cow.

Cat and mouse.

The bull and the goat in the first picture are quite often found together as a pair. However, based on the fact that all the other sets were found with two of the same animal, I have paired them all that way. Marked with a red "Japan" stamp. 4.5" to 4.75". $30-35.

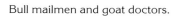

Bull mailmen and goat doctors.

Pig chefs and elephant policemen.

Shoeshine monkeys.

All of these dressed animals wear a vest and coat. Red "Germany" stamp. 3". $25-30.

Elephants and foxes.

Tigers and monkeys.

Owls and parrots.

Bears with fish. Marked with a paper "Japan" label. 2.75" to 3.5". $25-30.

Standing bears holding fish.

Sitting bear holding fish.

These sets feature a male and female. They are marked "Cooks Bazaar–Taiwan." 4" to 4.75". $12-15.

Squirrels and rabbits.

Pigs and bears.

A "Norcrest" label is on these sets. 3.5" to 4". $8-10.

Rabbits and cats.

Cattle and pigs.

30

Tall dressed animals are featured here. They have a red and gold "Made in Japan" label. 6". $25-30.

Cats and mice.

Dogs.

Foxes and rabbits.

Rabbits.

Smaller dressed animals. Marked with a "Takahashi–Japan." label. 2.75" to 3". $8-10.

Cats.

Bears.

These dressed lady animals are marked "Otagari–Japan." 4" to 4.25". $12-15.

Mice and bears.

Pigs and cats.

Here we have dressed couples. I am not sure if the horses with musical instruments really belong to this group, but coloring on the sets and marks are the same. Stamped "Japan." 3.75". $18-20.

Elephants and dogs.

Horses and cattle.

Animals playing leap-frog. Marked with a red "Japan" stamp. 4.5" as shown.
Duck set: $18-20. Others: $15-18.

Bears and pigs.

Ducks and monkeys.

This group is called "Weiner Dudes." Marked with a "Vandor–Taiwan" label. 2.75" to 3.75". $15-18.

Dog on surfboard, female dancer (stacker), and dog with a tire.

Animal musicians. Black "Japan" stamp. 4.5". $22-25.

Squirrel with cello, monkey with drum, and duck with saxophone.

A frog band. Blue "Japan" label. 2.5". $10-12.

Playing a drum and a banjo.

One pair plays a flute and a violin while the other pair plays an accordion and a saxophone.

Animals in or on Objects

Watering can animals. These are all in cans with a plain spout. They usually carry a "Japan" label. 2.5" to 3". $12-15.

Deer.

Cats and cows.

Chickens and giraffes.

Birds and black and white dogs.

Pigs and brown and white dogs.

Cats and a different pair of deer.

More watering can animals. On these, the spout has a knob at the end. Usually found with a blue and white "Japan" label. 2.5" to 3".
$12-15.

Deer.

Pigs and monkeys.

35

Chickens and giraffes.

Black and white dogs and cows.

Teapot animals. These teapots have a curved spout. Marked with a blue and white "Japan" label. 2.5" to 3.25". $15-18.

Dogs.

Ducks and chickens.

Cats on different bases and wearing a ribbon or bow tie on their necks. Red and gold "Japan" label. 3.25". $10-12.

Dogs and cats sitting on pillows. "Brinn's–Japan" label and stamped "T2133." 3" to 3.5". $8-10.

Cocker Spaniels and Poodles.

Two kinds of cats.

Animals in vegetable cars. Some of these pairs do not seem to go together, but they are shown as they were found. They are incised "Japan" but may also carry a sticker that reads "Manufactured for COTRIN LTD, MONTREAL." 3.5". $10-12.

Bear in mushroom and squirrel in cucumber.

Monkey in asparagus and cat in eggplant.

Pig in corn and rabbit in carrot.

Animals in cars. These have cold paint on the wheels and a smooth front. There is a great deal of discussion as to what is a proper pair. The animals in the cars are probably interchangeable. Black "Japan" stamp or a blue and white "Japan" label. 3" to 3.5". $20-25.

Cow and bull.

Pig and bear.

More animals in cars. These are made with a ribbed front and fired paint. Some have a blue and white "Japan" label while others have a black "Japan" stamp. As before, there is a question of proper pairings. 3" to 3.5". $20-25.

Rabbit.

Bear and opossum.

Dog and cow.

Animals in holders. "Josef Originals" and "Korea" on separate labels. 3.75"
to the top of the handle. $15-18.

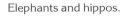
Elephants and hippos.

Pigs.

Ducks and chickens.

Animals in baskets with a bow. Incised "Japan." 3.5". $6-8.

Chickens.

Dogs and cats.

More animals in baskets. 3.5". $8-10.

Chickens and ducks.

Cows and rabbits.

These animals sit in a wicker-look basket. Some are labeled "Takahashi–Japan" while others have a "Distributed by Amrams–Toronto" label. 4". $10-12.

Pandas and brown bears.

Two different kinds of cats.

These animals stand in the baskets pictured. Each female has a pink flower on her head. Black and white "Japan" label. 3" to 3.5". $10-12.

Dogs.

Mice.

Cats.

These animals sit in the lined basket shown behind the set. They have a gold and black "Made in Korea" label. 2.25". $8-10.

Bears.

Dogs and cats.

Chicks in egg shells and pigs.

Woodland creature stackers. Green "Japan" stamp. 4.75" to 5". $15-18.

Elf on mushroom and frog on lily pad.

Rabbit on stump and owl on a different stump.

Circus animals. Gold "Quality–Japan" label. 4.5" to 5". $12-15.

Monkey on drum and lion on a different drum.

Elephant on circus stand.

Animals sitting on a bell base that says "Ring for Dinner." Blue and white "Japan" label. 3.5" to 4". $10-12.

Squirrels.

Fish and pelicans.

Bears and dogs.

These one piece animals are dressed. They have a "Napco–Japan" label and are also marked with "K15776." 7" long. $25-30.

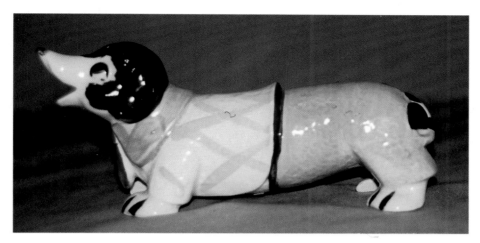

Dog.

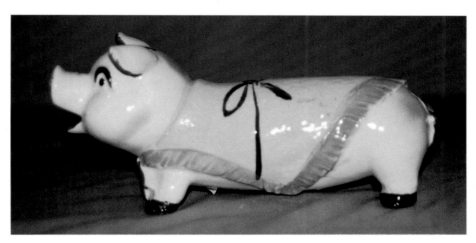

Pig.

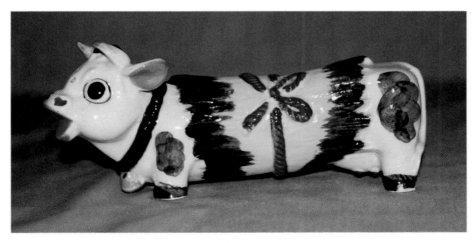

Cow.

These animals are marked with a black wreath emblem and "Japan." 8.5" to 9.5". $25-30.

Alligator.

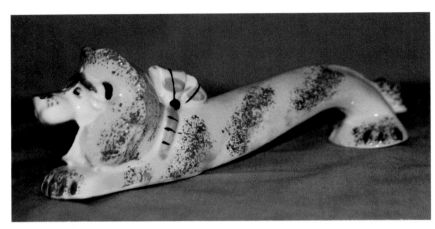

Lion.

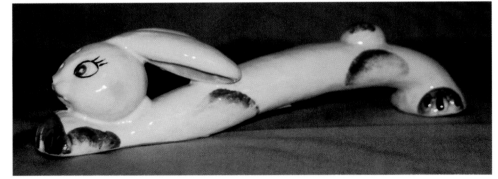

Rabbit.

Fox.

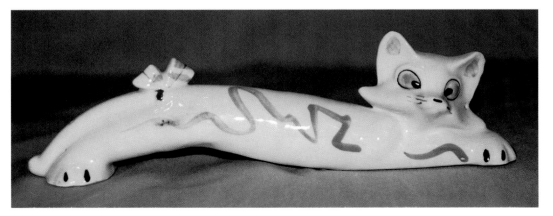

Cat.

Dog, sometimes called "Tramp" from *Lady and the Tramp*.

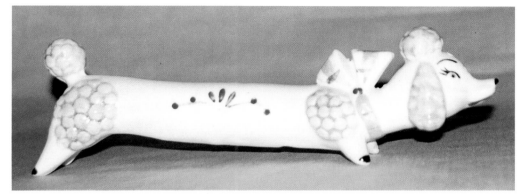

Poodle.

Stitched, Sewn, Mosaic, and Tall Animals

All of these animals are marked with an "S" and "P" on the front. They have a blue and white "Japan" paper label. 3.25" to 3.5". $10-12.

Pigs.

Bears and dogs.

Hippos and elephants.

Gingham and calico animals. Marked with an "N" inside a "C" but no country. 2.5" to 3". $10-12.

Elephants and donkeys.

Cats and dogs.

Tall stitched animals with "S" and "P" on the front. Blue and white "Japan" paper label. 7.75". $12-15.

Right: Cats.

Far right: Poodles and elephants.

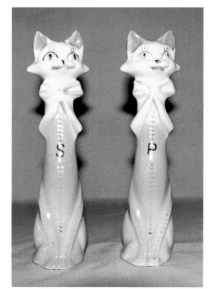

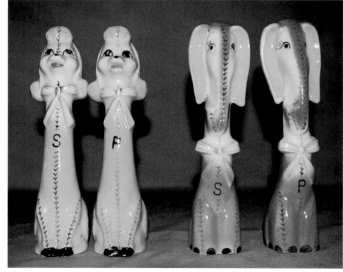

White animals with a mosaic design. Marked "Relco–Japan." 4.5" to 5.25". $10-12.

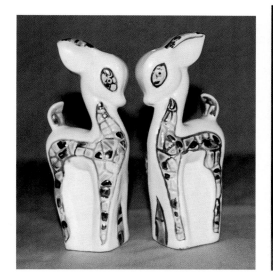

Deer.

Giraffes and elephants.

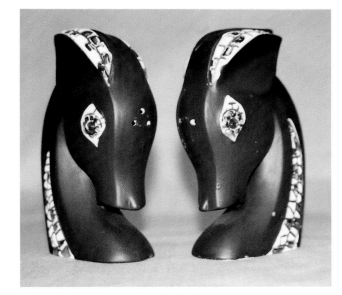

Brown animal heads with mosaic trim. 4.75". $8-10.

Left:
Deer.

Bottom left:
Horses.

Giraffes.

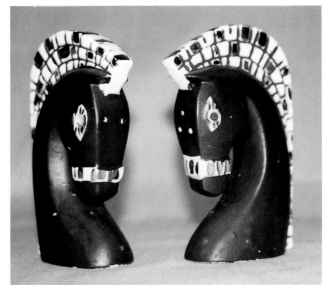

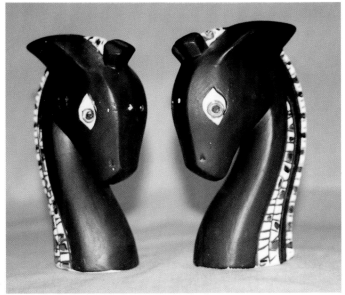

53

Tall boys with "S" and "P" on the front. Black "Napco" stamp and "K2698." 8.5" to 9". $12-15.

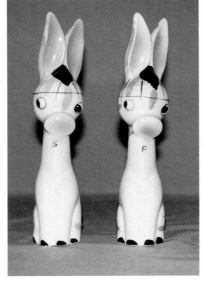

Donkeys.

Dogs and cats.

Zebras and giraffes.

More tall animals, this time a male and female. The mice are marked "Norcrest" while the others have a black "Japan" stamp. 6.5" to 6.75". $15-18.

Lambs and poodles.

Mice and skunks.

Rabbits and bears.

Tall boys wearing hats or ribbons. They have a "Napco–Japan" label and are marked with numbers. Also, each is stamped with a name on the bottom. 8" to 8.5". $18-20.

Marked "Kitten."

Marked "Duck" and "Bunny."

Marked "Reindeer" and "Bambi."

Single shaker marked "Dog."

Other Animals

Bunnies in different modes of transport. These were designed as Easter sets. They are marked with "OCI–China." 3". $12-15.

On the train.

In the car.

Animals with moveable eyes. They have a blue and white "Japan" label or a black "Japan" stamp. 1.25" to 3.75". $8-10.

Monkeys and owls.

Dogs and bears.

Squirrels and cats.

Moose and alligators.

Moms carrying babies. Marked "Napco–Japan." 3.75" to 4.5". Monkey: $15-18. Others: $12-15.

Kangaroos.

Monkeys and bears.

Let's play. Marked with an "Enesco–Taiwan" label. 3" to 3.5". $8-10.

Rabbits.

Cats and dogs.

One animal lying on the other makes up this series. Marked with a "New Trends–Made in Japan" label. 3" to 3.75". $10-12.

Bears and mice.

Monkeys and dogs.

These hat wearing animals are marked with a black "Germany" stamp. 2.75". $15-18.

Dogs and pigs.

Elephants.

Pigs and donkeys.

Animals in strange colors. As you can see by the two pairs of owls, they were also made in different colors from the same mold. Marked with a black "Japan" stamp. 3.25" to 3.5". $3-5.

Cats.

Owls.

More animals made in strange colors. These have some accent color on the feet and ears. These were also made in different colors from the same mold. Marked with a blue "Japan" stamp. 3.5". $4-6.

Monkeys and cats.

Bears in two colors.

Bulls and cows.

Monkeys and cows.

An embossed design is common to these sets. They carry an "Enesco–Japan" label. 3.25" to 3.5". $5-7.

Elephants and owls.

64

Pigs.

Cats and donkeys.

Here we have some male and female animals heads. Green "Japan" stamp. 3". $12-15.

Poodles.

Lambs.

Bears.

Elephants.

Cats.

Dogs.

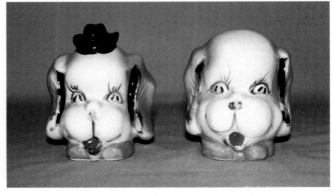

65

In these sets, the swinger is a shaker and the base is the other shaker. They are marked with "Pat.T.T." on the bottom. $25-30.

Birds and a single dog.

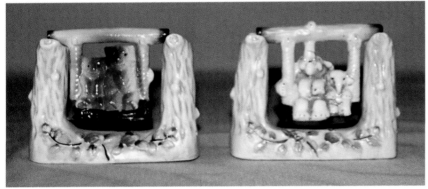

Bears and elephants.

These brightly colored animals are made of a strange composition-like material. They carry no marks but are all stamped with "E-9899." 1.5". $4-6.

Possums?

Elephants and hippos.

Skunks and turtles.

A "gingerbread" decoration is on the head of each of these animals. They have a red "Japan" stamp. 2.5" to 3.25". $5-7.

Elephants.

Skunks and squirrels.

Deer and raccoons.

Donkeys and cows.

Sheep and rabbits.

Cats in two poses.

White animals with blue and gold accents. Some have a red "Japan" stamp and some have a black "Japan" stamp. 2.25" to 3". $5-7.

Dogs and cats.

Pigs and chickens.

Penguins and bears.

Animals dressed in related objects. Stamped "CA" (for Clay Art) and a paper label reading "Made in the Philippines." 4". $12-15.

Cats in fish and bird; dogs in fire hydrant and wiener bun.

Cows in ice cream cone and bottle of milk; pigs in ear of corn and watermelon.

The hang tags that came with these sets declare that they are "The Inseparable Pairs." Made for Enesco. 3.25" to 4" for the pair on the bench. $10-12.

Male bear and chair are shakers, girl bear is toothpick holder.

Bears on bench and bears with bowls.

Sports animals. They have a black "Japan" stamp. 5". $18-20.

Racing rabbits.

Weightlifting bears.

Bowling (or maybe soccer) dogs

These plastic animals were intended to be used in the lunch box, according to the packaging on one of the sets I purchased. They were made in Hong Kong. 2". $3-5.

Rabbits and yellow dogs.

Mice and cats.

Gray dogs and lions.

Owls and monkeys.

Natural Looking Birds and Fish

Birds sitting on tree stumps. "Victoria Ceramics–Japan" label. 3" to 3.75". $10-12.

Red-headed Woodpeckers and Robins.

Orioles and Cardinals.

Birds on a pedestal-like base. Green "Japan" stamp. 3.25". $12-15.

Blue Jays.

Parakeets and Robins.

Birds sitting on trays. These are marked with a black "Made in Japan" stamp. 2.5" to 3". $10-12.

Ducks and unidentified species.

Red-winged Blackbirds and Red-headed Woodpeckers.

Goldfinches and Flickers.

Small birds. "Made in Japan" paper label. 1.25" to 2". Parakeet and hummingbird: $10-12. All others: $8-10.

Two unrecognized species.

Cardinals and Blue Jays.

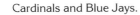

Parakeets and Hummingbirds.

73

Birds sitting on logs. They are stamped with the name of the bird on the bottom but have no other marks. 3.5". $10-12.

Bluebirds.

Blue Jays and Orioles.

Birds on leaves. Blue and white "Japan" label. 2.875" to 3.125". $10-12.

Cardinals and Goldfinches.

Blue Jays and Cedar Waxwings.

Swans with flowers on their backs. Marked "Royal Adderley Bone China– England." 2". $12-15.

Various kinds of ducks, probably made from the same mold. This mold has a smooth back. They have an "Enesco–Japan" paper label. 3". $8-10.

More ducks, this time you can see the feathers on the back. Again, I feel these are also made from the same mold. They have an "Enesco–Japan" paper label. 3". $8-10.

Plastic ducks. No marks 1.5" $3-5.

This series of stoneware fish on rocks was created by Idaho artist Don Mintz and made in the United States. 3.25" to 4". $35-$40.

Brook trout.

Walleye.

Brown trout.

Rainbow trout.

Largemouth bass.

Northern pike.

Bluegill.

Chinook salmon.

Salmon.

Bisque finish fish with the name of the fish written in script on the bottom along with the number "3241" and "Enesco–Japan." 3.25" to 3.5". $18-20.

Northern pike.

Pickerel.

Sunfish.

Rainbow trout.

Black bass.

Fish with names stamped on them. All are marked "PY" and have a "Ucagco–Japan" label. 2" to 2.5". Swordfish: $30-35. All others: $25-30.

Sea drum and smallmouth bass.

Rainbow trout.

Brook trout and sword-fish.

Sunfish.

Silver perch.

Common pompano.

Red snapper.

Fish without names. Marked "PY" and have a "Ucagco–Japan" label. 2" to 3". $22-25.

More fish with names stamped on them. "Relco–Japan" label. 1.5" to 3.25". $18-20.

Yellow perch.

Bullheads and brown trout.

Walleyed pike and rainbow trout.

Bluegills and rock bass.

Smallmouth black bass and muskellunge.

Large tropical fish. Marked "PY" and some have a "Ucagco–Japan" label. 3.5" to 4.25". $22-25.

Striped fish, one shaker in each pair is pink/blue and the other is pink/black in color. Black "Japan" stamp. 3" to 3.5". $15-18.

Other Birds, Fish, and Various Creatures

Dressed penguins. Green "Japan" stamp. 3.75". $15-18.

Ice skating and golfing.

Captain and mate; strolling male and female.

Male and female birds with big eyes wearing hats. Green "Japan" stamp. 4.5". $6-8.

Chickens and owls.

Penguin chefs and Bluebirds.

Dressed ducks in three poses. Black or green "Japan" stamp. 5.5". $18-20.

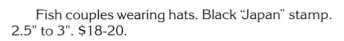

Fish couples wearing hats. Black "Japan" stamp. 2.5" to 3". $18-20.

More fish couples wearing hats. The first pair looks like a bride and groom. "Sonsco–Japan" label. 2.5" to 3". $12-15.

Fish with faces. Stamped "Japan." 2.75" to 4". $22-25.

Different kinds of shells. Marked "PY" but some also had a "Napco–Japan" label. 1" to 1.5". $15-18.

Cowrie and turban.

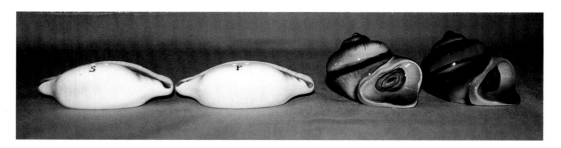

Nutmeg and turban.

Cone and unknown type.

Sea creatures with bodies. Blue and white "Japan" label. 2" to 2.25". $35-40.

Seahorses.

Lobsters and crabs.

Sting rays and fish.

Different kinds of dinosaurs. Marked "Takahashi–Japan. 1.75" to 2.5". $15-18.

Triceratops.

Brontosaurus and stegosaurus.

Tyrannosaurus.

These dinosaurs have intertwined necks. The name of the dinosaur is stamped on the bottom of the set. They have a blue and white "Japan" label. 4" to 4.25". $45-50.

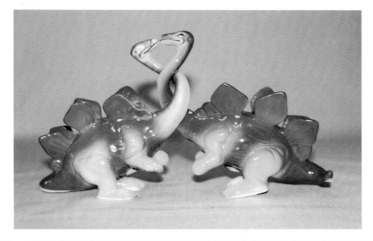

Stegosaurus.

Iguanodon.

Brontosaurus.

Water related creatures carrying umbrellas. Green "Japan" stamp. 3.5" to 4". $10-12.

Ducks.

Penguins and seals.

Flowers

Flowers with faces. Because of the faces, I am not attempting to identify the kind of flower represented. Marked "PY." 3". $30-35.

These bone china eggs were made by the Sandford Company of England. Where the design is different on each side, the egg is turned to show both sides. The egg with the large poinsettia in the fifth picture is blank on the back. The strawberries and blossoms in the first picture may not belong to the series, but I included them anyway. 2". $12-15.

Strawberries and blossoms.

Thistle and a Scotch flower of some kind.

Purple thistle and violets.

Blue roses and forget-me-nots.

Two sizes of poinsettias.

Two colors and sizes of roses.

Red roses and dogwood.

In this group of flowers, one shaker has been turned so that the back of the shaker is shown. They have a "Lefton–Japan" label and also have the number "4474" stamped on the sets. 3.25". $10-12.

Blue and white flowers.

Red flowers and pansies.

Sunflowers and violets.

Fruit and Vegetables

These sets are stamped "PY" and also carry a "Ucagco–Japan" label. 2.25" to 3". $12-15.

Strawberries and watermelons.

Carrots and tomatoes.

Stacking baskets of vegetables. The basket is one shaker, the vegetables the other. Marked "Mann–1982." 4". $8-10.

Green peppers and eggplants.

Cauliflower and tomatoes.

Brightly colored vegetables. In these pictures, one vegetable is turned on its side to show the top detail better. Blue and white "Japan" label. 4" to 4.5" long. $6-8.

Green peppers.

Carrots and radishes.

Chinese cabbage and eggplants.

Long, one piece vegetables. No marks. 8.25" to 9" long. $15-18.

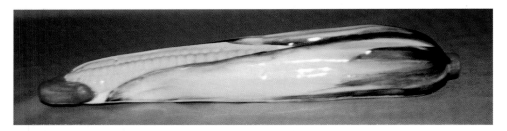

An ear of corn.

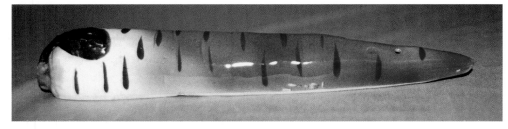

Radish.

Lima beans.

Chinese cabbage.

Pairs of long vegetables which closely resemble the one piece vegetables in the previous pictures. Blue & white "Japan" label. 8.5" to 8.75" long. $12-15.

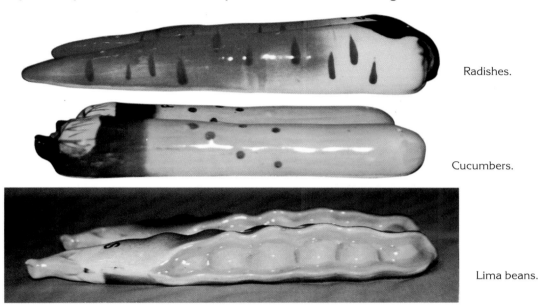

Radishes.

Cucumbers.

Lima beans.

Vegetables with insects on them. Green "Japan" stamp. 1.25" to 2". $15-18.

Tomatoes.

Front of green pepper with a red pepper and a pair of turnips.

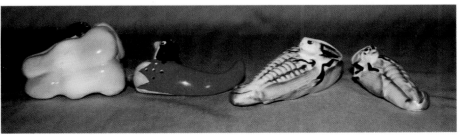

Back of green pepper with a red pepper and ears of corn.

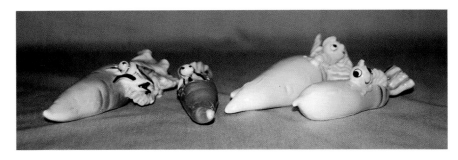

Carrots and white radishes.

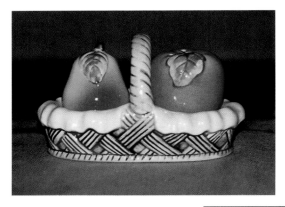

Vegetables and fruit in low baskets. Have "Josef Original" and "Korea" on separate labels. 2.75" to the top of the handle. $12-15.

Pear and apple.

A tomato with a green pepper and asparagus with an eggplant.

Baskets of fruit packed in balsa crates. The second picture shows the white basket at the bottom which is common to all the sets. "Enesco–Japan" label. 2.5" to the top of the crate. $6-8.

Grapes and lemons.

Strawberries and green apples.

These plastic fruit are packed in plastic crates. Except for the pair of apples, each crate is marked with the kind of fruit it contains. Marked "Made in Hong Kong." 2.25". $3-5.

Above right:
Lemons and oranges.

Right:
Apples and pineapples.

Anthropomorphic

Fruit heads wearing something on their heads. Stamped "PY" and "Japan." 3" to 3.5". $30-35.

Oranges and apples.

Watermelons and pineapples.

Pears and strawberries.

Fruit heads wearing hats. These have a "Napco–Japan" label. They appear to be of "PY" quality, but are not marked as such. 3" to 3.5". $25-28.

Peaches and oranges.

Pears and grapes.

Shakers on wires stands. "Dabs–Japan" label. 3.75" to 5.5" $70-75.

Cabbage and beet.

Cucumber and carrot.

Golf club and golf ball.

In this group, three of the sets are playing instruments, while the other three appear to be listening to the concert. "Japan" paper label. The mate to the single shown in the second photo appears to be a peach. The pair can be seen on page 120 of Helene Guarnaccia's fourth book. Black "Japan" stamp. 3" to 3.5". $45-50.

Apple with strawberry and cantaloupe with eggplant.

Watermelon with red pepper and a single pineapple (peach mate plays accordion).

Orange with cherries and pear with grapes.

More musicians. They have a "Japan" paper label. 3.75" to 4". $30-35.

Onions playing the violin.

Peaches playing lyre and cantaloupes playing accordion.

101

Eggplants singing and a single lima bean playing the cello.

Limes? playing the banjo.

Fruit and vegetable heads wearing collars. Black "Japan" stamp. 2.5" to 3". $35-40.

Figs and blueberries.

Potatoes and apples.

Pears and peaches.

Standing fruit. Green "Japan" stamp. 4". $20-22.

Pears.   Cantaloupes and peaches.

More fruit people. Black "Japan" stamp. 3". $18-20.

Apples and peaches.

Cantaloupes and pears.

Vegetables with feet. "Sonsco–Japan" label or a green "Japan" stamp. 3.75" to 4". $22-25.

Chinese cabbage with celery.

Cucumber with green pepper and carrot with white radish.

Sitting vegetable people. Black "Japan" stamp. 4". $35-40.

Sweet potato with a turnip.

Peas with a carrot and an ear of corn with a pineapple.

Boy tomato and boy Chinese cabbage.

Girl cabbage with boy corn and girl lettuce with boy beet.

Brightly colored vegetable people. In this series, the bottom of the shakers is painted the same color as the color nearest the bottom. They have either a black "Japan" stamp or a "Japan" paper label. 3.5" to 3.75". $28-30.

Sitting polka dot vegetables. Black "Japan" stamp. 3" to 3.5". $25-28.

Eggplants and carrots.

Chinese cabbage.

Cucumbers and peas.

Sweet potatoes and pumpkins.

Green peppers.

This picture shows a single shaker from each of the twelve sets making up the entire series, part of which is pictured on the previous page. Each set has one shaker with two holes and one shaker with three holes.

The entire series.

Fruit with moveable eyes sitting on leaves. These are stackers, with the fruit being a shaker and the leaf being the other shaker. Stamped "Japan." 2.5" to 3.25". $30-35.

An orange? and a watermelon.

A peach, a pear, and an apple.

Fruit heads. The back of the head is shaped as the fruit would be. Black "Japan" stamp. 1.75" to 2.5". $15-18.

Strawberries and peaches.

Oranges and cantaloupes.

Apples and grapes.

Figs and pineapples.

Fruit and vegetables in different kinds of baskets. Blue "Japan" stamp. 3.5" to 3.75". $12-15.

Lemons and green peppers.

Bananas and pineapples.

Pears and apples.

More fruit and vegetables, this time in the same kind of basket. Black "Japan" stamp. 3" to 3.5". $12-15.

Green apples.

Green peppers and peaches.

Standing vegetables wearing shoes. Incised "Japan." 4.5" to 4.75". $6-8.

Mushrooms and eggplants.

Ears of corn and green peppers.

Cucumbers and carrots.

Sitting vegetables, all dressed in red and wearing shoes. Black "Japan" stamp. 4.25" to 4.5". $18-20.

Mushrooms.

Ears of corn and Chinese cabbage.

Pineapples and peanuts.

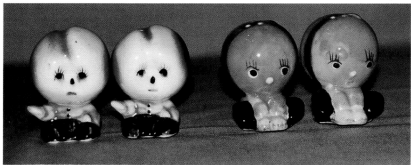

Sitting fruit and vegetables. Black "Japan" stamp or a blue and white "Japan" label. 2.5" to 2.75". $10-12.

Peaches and watermelons.

Green grapes and purple grapes.

Apples and strawberries.

Eggplants and turnips.

Fruit and vegetable faces with strange eyes. Each shaker has the same number of holes. This may have been a case of "mix and match." One set is marked "Lipper and Mann." The other sets are unmarked. 3" to 3.5". $12-15.

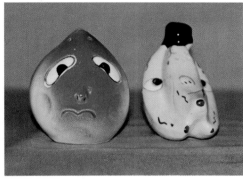

Above left:
Celery with a beet.

Above:
An onion with garlic.

Far left:
An apple with a pear.

Left:
A peach with a bunch of bananas.

Boy and girl fruit with moveable eyes. Another set in this series is watermelons. 3.25" to 3.5". $25-30.

Plums?

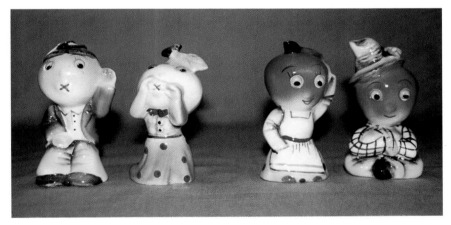

Pears and apples.

Mushrooms with collars. Marked "PY." 2.5". $20-25.

111

People

Clowns

These clowns have a "Lefton–Japan" label. 4" to 6". $25-30.

Clowns playing leapfrog.

Clown with goose dressed as a clown.

One clown is right side up, the other is upside down.

Turnabout clowns showing happy and sad faces. "Napco–Japan" label. 4" to 4.25". $22-25.

Clowns with happy faces.

Reverse side of clowns in previous picture, now with sad faces.

Upside down clowns with happy faces.

Reverse side of clowns in previous picture, showing sad faces.

Clowns in polka dot outfits. Red "Made in Japan" stamp. 2.75" to 3.5". $18-20.

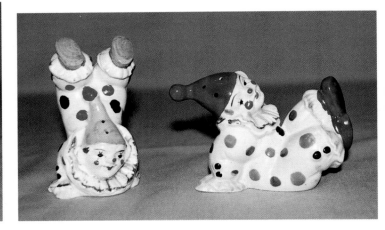

Performing clowns. Green "Japan" stamp. 2.5" for the separate ones to 6.5" for the stackers. $22-25.

International

"Kissers" from different countries. Some have a hang tag telling their country. They are shown facing forward and then in a "kissing" position. Black and white "Japan" label. 4.25" to 4.5". $12-15.

Japanese and Mexican couples facing forward.

Japanese and Mexican couples kissing.

German? and Scottish couples facing forward.

German and Scottish couples kissing.

115

Kissing children holding objects behind their backs. "Enesco–Japan" label. 3". $10-12.

Oriental boy with umbrella and girl with hat;
Dutch boy with boat and girl with tulip.

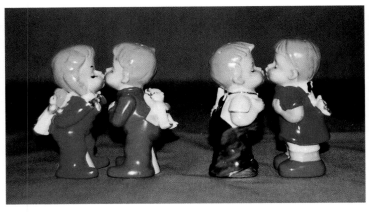

Girl holds doll while boy holds teddy bear; boy holds sling
shot and girl holds flower. Both Americans?

Children from different countries. "Made in Taiwan" label. 3.5" to 4". $8-10.

Orientals.

American Indians and Africans.

Hawaiians and Dutch.

European kissing couples. Marked with a green "Japan" stamp. 4.5" to 5". $12-15.

These sets carry no marks, but it is believed that they are American made. 3.75" to 4.75". $12-15.

American cowboys and American Indians.

Scotland and Switzerland.

Chefs from different countries. The tray of food is a shaker and the set is shown both together and separately. Marked with a "Clay Art–Made in China." label. 3.875" to 4.5". $12-15.

Mexican chef holding tray.

Mexican chef with tray shown separately.

Japanese chef holding tray.

Japanese chef with tray shown separately.

Italian chef holding tray.

Italian chef with tray shown separately.

Farmers and a farmer's wife. Although not marked, they were made in Thailand for the Oriental Ceramics Co., an English firm. 3.75" to 4.25". $15-18.

The farmer with a cow and the farmer with a sheep.

The farmer with a pig and the farmer's wife with a chicken.

These sets of occupations were also made in Thailand for the Oriental Ceramics Co. Again, they are not marked. 4" to 5". $15-18.

An Eskimo with a seal.

The postman with a mailbox and the blacksmith with his anvil.

A policeman with a crook and female and male traffic wardens.

A lobster fisherman with his lobster trap and an angler with his creel.

120

Angels playing instruments. Note that each instrument has a bird perched on it. They have a "Lefton–Japan" label and are marked with the number "2011." 3.75". $22-25.

Cello player and flute player.

Lyre player with horn player and cello player with flute player.

Tuba players.

More angel musicians. Green "Japan" stamp. 3" to 3.5". $10-12.

Angels holding music books and accordion players.

People in Sports

These fellows are all on the same type of base. Marked with an "Enesco–Japan" label. 4" to 4.5". $20-25.

Football players.

Baseball players and boxers.

These babies in blue diapers are into sports. "Enesco–Japan" label. 4.25". $15-18.

Boxers.

Baseball players and tennis players.

Children playing football. No marks. 3". $18-20.

Young boxers. Black "Japan" stamp. 3.25". $18-20.

More sports players. These have an "OCI–Taiwan" label. 4". $12-15.

Golfers and tennis players.

Football and baseball players.

These red-nosed fellows also like sports. Their jerseys have "S" and "P" in place of numbers on the back. They are stamped "Napco," "1958," and "IC3124," on the bottom of the sets. 3.75". $20-22.

Football players.

Basketball and baseball players.

Other People

A card that was enclosed with one of the following sets calls these sets "Ambassadors of Good Cheer" and "The Human Race in Satire." Each set is a satirical depiction of a zodiac sign. They have a red "Japan" stamp. 4.5". $35-40.

The ram for Aries and the bull for Taurus.

The twins for Gemini and the crab for Cancer.

The lion for Leo and the virgin for Virgo.

The clown for Libra and the scorpion for Scorpio.

The detective for Sagittarius and the goat for Capricorn.

The water boy for Aquarius and the fish for Pisces.

It is reported that these sets represent famous people. I am listing the names of the sets as they were told to me. They are marked "Imported Exclusively by Abbott–Japan." 3.5". $30-35.

Marie Antoinette.

Cleopatra.

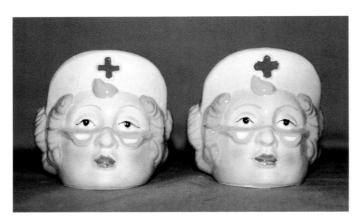

Clara Barton.

Chef Pierre.

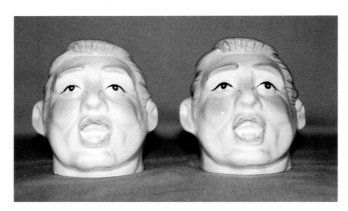

Tarzan.

William Shakespeare.

Angels of the month. July is missing. They have a red and gold "Artmark–Japan" label. 3.75". $25-30.

January and February.

March and April.

May and June.

August only.

September and October.

November and December.

Kappas. The Kappa is part of Japanese folklore. It is said that his presence will bring everlasting joy and luck to the person who gazes upon his image. Marked "A Quality Product—Japan." 3.75". $35-40.

Kappas shown facing forward.

Two other Kappas facing forward.

Two sets of Kappas placed so that the bases fit together.

David the Gnome. The set of David and his wife was issued later than the other three and may not belong to the series. Marked "Uniebock B.V." (Netherlands). 4" to 5". $65-75.

David with his granddaughter and David with a rabbit.

David with a squirrel and David with his wife.

Elves and animals. Stamped "Shafford–Japan." 4". $22-25.

Deer and elf.

Giraffe and elf with ladder.

Donkey and elf.

Bisque looking elves. "Taiwan" label and stamped "88241." 2.5" to 3.5". $15-18.

Elves with baskets and elves with beards.

Elves carrying jugs and chef elves.

These Santas with handlebar mustaches appear to be carrying very heavy loads. "Japan" label. 4.25" to 5". $18-20.

Santa with another Santa on his back.

Santa with Mrs. Santa on his back and Santa with a pack of toys on his back.

Colonial type busts. Each couple wears different hats. I feel that a proper match has the same color band on the base. Green "Japan" stamp. 4". $10-12.

Heads with a blue band around base.

Heads with a pink band around base.

Heads with a green band around base.

Couples with flowers on their heads. On close inspection, it appears that they represent the seasons of the year. 4.25". $15-18.

Winter and Spring.

Summer and Fall.

Formally dressed couples with fork and spoon heads. No marks. 5". $40-45.

Couples dancing the waltz and the mamba.

He proposes to her (Be Mine?) and the wedding day.

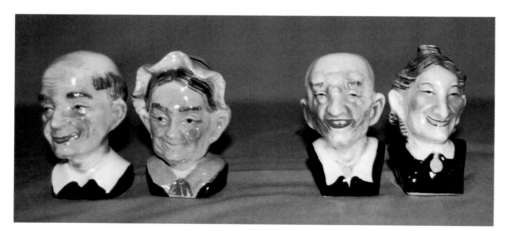

These strange pairs of heads do not always look like a man and woman. Based on their hair styles, it has been determined that they are. These sets have a rectangular shaped base. Green "Japan" stamp. 2.75" to 3.25". $8-10.

Travel

These sets were marketed as "American Souvenirs." Some of the sets were given names. I have indicated the name in either parentheses or quotation marks. They carry a "Papel-Freelance–Sri Lanka" label. 2" to 4.25". $12-15.

Indian and teepee (Pow wow).

Empire State Building and taxi (Downtown).

Cow singer with bull musician (Moo-dy Blues) and cowboy boots with hat.

Lobster with shell (Seaside) and chili pepper with cactus (Red hot).

"Gators on the Go" and " Snow Bunnies."

"Traveling America" is the title of this series. They have a "Hand Painted–Dept. 56–Japan" label. 2.5" to 5.5" $15-18.

Roll of film with camera and tent with car.

Car with map and stacking camping lantern.

The holes on the top of these split scenes make an "S" and "P" and are painted black. I am sure there are many others that we did not locate. They have a black "Japan" stamp. 3". $15-18.

Crater Lake, Oregon.

Bonneville Dam, Oregon.

Mt. Hood, Oregon.

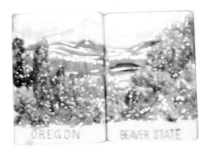

Oregon, Beaver State.

Mt. Rainier, Washington.

Grand Canyon Nat'l Park.

Old Faithful, Yellowstone Park.

Niagara Falls, Canada.

Country Store, Phoenix, Arizona.

The Grotto of the Blessed Virgin Mary.

Juarez, Mexico.

Ready-To-Eat Food

These sets are called "Apple Delite." Stamped "Omnibus–China." 3" to 3.5". $12-15.

This "Clam Bake" series is also stamped "Omnibus–China." 1.5" to 3". $12-15.

Jelly and preserves.

Corn on the cob.

Cookbooks.

Clams on a plate with lemon slices.

Granny Smith and Macintosh apples.

Crabs.

Breakfast is served. Licensed by Nick & Nora–New York. Stamped "Vandor–China." 2.5" to 3". $12-15.

Pancake mix with syrup in a log cabin bottle and an orange half with a juicer.

Chocolate and white milk in bottles and an egg in an egg cup with a slice of toast.

Desserts made by Cardinal, Inc. Stamped "CI–China." 1.5" to 2.5". $10-12.

Ice cream sandwich with a strawberry tart and a chocolate eclair with a strawberry cream tart.

Chocolate sundae with mixed fruit tart and chocolate bon-bon cake with a rectangular piece of chocolate cake. The cake has a pink icing flower on top.

A wedge of yellow cake with a petit four and a blueberry pie with chocolate layer cake.

Shopping carts filled with good things to eat. "Applause, Inc.–Made in Thailand" label. Cart is 5.5" high. Shakers from 2.5" to 3.5" $12-15.

Far left:
Cookies and milk.

Left:
Peanut butter and jelly.

Far left:
Whipped cream and a box of strawberries.

Left:
Pepper and salt.

Condiments and Three Piece Sets

These fish condiments were probably made in Japan although they are not marked. 3.75". $30-35.

A green fish condiment.

A red fish condiment.

A green fish condiment.

Split dogs wrapped around a mustard fire hydrant. The dachshunds say "Hi Friend" in raised letters along their sides. All were made in Japan. 4". Dachshunds: $15-18. All others: $20-25.

Schnauzer.

Gray Dachshund.

Brown Dachshund.

Poodle.

Fish condiments made of heavy pottery. Some were marked "Portugal." 3.5" to 4.5". $45-50.

These three piece sets feature a toothpick holder as the third piece and all are on trays. They are incised "Japan." 3.25". $6-8.

Dogs.

Mice.

Owls.

Miscellaneous

This display features Coca-Cola ® products. 2" to 3.5" when stacked. $13-15 per set. $125 for the complete set with the rack.

The entire display on its rack.

Stacked fountain dispenser and a six pack of bottles.

The previous picture showing the pairs separated.

Two kinds of stacked bottle dispensing machines.

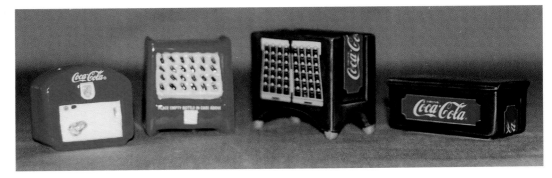

The previous picture showing the pairs separated.

Delivery man and delivery truck.

The previous picture showing the pairs separated.

155

Lighthouses marked "Young's Inc–China." 4.25". $10-12.

Stacking lighthouses. Marked "Ganz–Taiwan." 4.75" $12-15.

A teapot series marked "OCI–China." 3" to 3.5". $15-18.

Lighthouses and library cats.

Market place carts and picnic baskets.

Tailor shop and Mama's kitchen.

Market flowers and fruit; Harvest (corn and asparagus).

Anthropomorphic fire engines with other vehicles. Marked "Japan." 2" to 2.25". $40-45.

Bus and a fire engine with a boot on top.

Locomotive and a fire engine with hose on top.

Street car and a fire engine with helmet on top.

Houshould items that remind us of the '50s. Marked "Omnibus–China." 2.5" to 4". $12-15.

Table with telephone and sweeper.

Basket of clothes and laundry supplies.

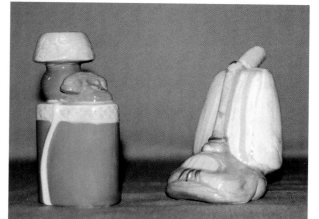

Cup of coffee and coffee pot.

Tea kettle and cooking pan.

"Cookies to Market" is the name of this series. The shakers are patterned after cookie jars made during the '50s and '60s. "Dept. 56–Made in China" label. $15-18.

Boy pig with girl pig and lamb with chick.

Dutch girl and boy; Red Riding Hood with Grandmother.

Sports items. Since these carry two different markings and one is unmarked, I am not sure that they all belong together. I decided that they look enough alike to be included. The set in the first picture is unmarked. Those in the second picture have a "Giftcraft–Taiwan" label. Those in the last picture are marked "SDD–Korea." 4.125" to 5.5". $12-15.

Golf.

Baseball and bowling.

Soccer and tennis.

Bibliography

Davern, Melva. *The Collector's Encyclopedia of Salt & Pepper Shakers, Figural and Novelty*. Paducah, Ky: Collector Books, 1985.

Guarnaccia, Helene. *Salt & Pepper Shakers IV*. Paducah, Ky: Collector Books, 1985.